Robert E. Lee

MILITARY LEADERS OF THE CIVIL WAR

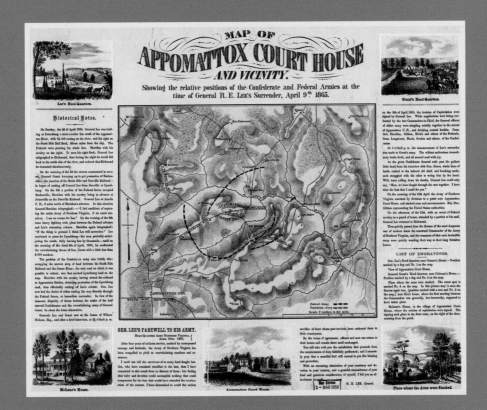

Don McLeese

Publishing LLC
Vero Beach, Florida 32964

© 2006 Rourke Publishing LLC

www.rourkepublishing.com

PHOTO CREDITS: p. 9 ©Getty Images; p. 20, 21 USMA Library; all other images from the Library of Congress

Title page: This illustration shows the position of Confederate and Union forces at the time of Lee's surrender.

Editor: Frank Sloan

Cover and page design by Nicola Stratford

Library of Congress Cataloging-in-Publication Data

McLeese, Don.
  Robert E. Lee / Don McLeese.
      p. cm. -- (Military leaders of the civil war)
  Includes index.
  ISBN 1-59515-476-0 (hardcover)
  1. Lee, Robert E. (Robert Edward), 1807-1870--Juvenile literature. 2. Generals--Confederate States of America--Biography--Juvenile literature. 3. Confederate States of America. Army--Biography--Juvenile literature. 4. United States--History--Civil War, 1861-1865--Campaigns--Juvenile literature. I. Title.
  E467.1.L4M49 2006
  973.7'3'092--dc22

                              2005010980

Printed in the USA

Rourke Publishing
1-800-394-7055
www.rourkepublishing.com
sales@rourkepublishing.com
Post Office Box 3328, Vero Beach, FL 32964

Table of Contents

~

A Great Hero

No Civil War **general** was a greater hero to the South than Robert E. Lee. He was a man who loved his country, the United States of America. But he also loved Virginia, the state where he was born.

When Virginia left the United States in 1861, it formed a new country with other Southern states called the **Confederate** States of America. The Northern states said that the South couldn't start its own country. The two sides fought the war to decide whether the United States would be one country or two.

An engraving that shows Robert E. Lee standing in his camp

Lee leads his troops during the Battle of Fredericksburg in 1862.

Robert E. Lee had been an officer in the U.S. army. He was known as one of the smartest, bravest, and best **soldiers**. But when Virginia left the United States, Robert left the U.S. army. He became the leader of the Confederate army. He hadn't wanted to turn against the United States. But he couldn't turn against his home state of Virginia.

Son of a General

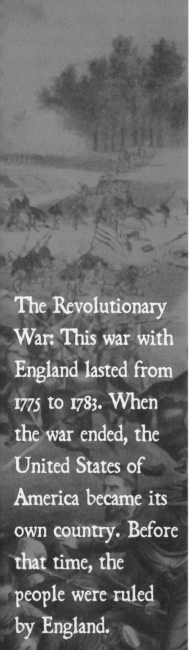

Robert Edward Lee was born on January 19, 1807. His father had also been a famous general and a war hero. His name was Harry Lee. He was known as "Light-Horse Harry," because of his bravery on horseback. He served with George Washington in the Revolutionary War. Henry was governor of the state of Virginia when he married Ann Hill Carter, Robert's mother.

Harry Lee was known as "Light-Horse Harry."

A typical plantation of the South

Stratford Hill

~

When Robert was born, his family lived in one of the finest houses in Virginia. It was a brick **mansion** on a **plantation** named Stratford Hill. Harry wasn't very good with money. When Robert was just two years old, his father was sent to prison for not paying his bills. When he got out the next year, the family moved to Alexandria, Virginia.

Robert's mother had relatives there, and they would help the Lee family with money. Robert's father moved away from the family in 1813, and he died when his son was just 11 years old.

Robert hadn't known his father very well, but he was very close to his mother. He loved her very much. She was often sick, and Robert tried to take care of her. She didn't want him to make the mistakes with money that his father had made.

A Very Good Student

~

Robert was one of the smartest students in his school. He loved to read and was very good with numbers. He went to school at the Alexandria Academy until he was 16.

Robert's mother knew he should go to college, but college cost a lot of money. Robert's family was very poor. There was one college that was free. It was called the United States **Military** Academy at West Point, New York. Because Robert was such a good student, the U.S. Military Academy admitted him.

Robert E. Lee is shown at the time he was a cadet at West Point.

At West Point

~

Robert traveled to West Point to begin his training in 1825. West Point only accepted the best students, and Robert was one of the best of the best. He was second in his class when he graduated in 1829.

West Point from the Hudson River

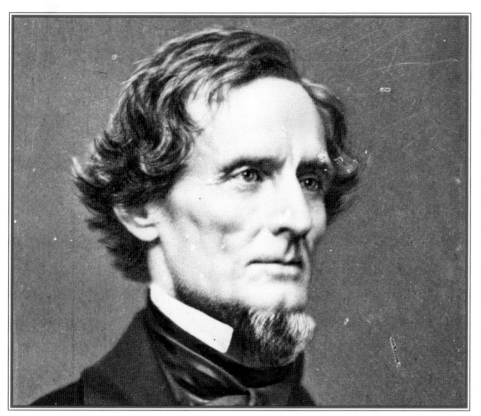

One of the cadets at West Point with Lee was Jefferson Davis.

He was also one of the best behaved. Students at West Point are called **cadets**. Whenever a cadet broke any rule at West Point, no matter how small, a mark was placed next to his name. This mark was called a **demerit**. Almost all of the cadets had demerits next to their names when they left West Point. Some of them had many of them. Robert never broke a single rule or received a single demerit.

15

An Engineer

~

The country was at peace when Robert left West Point, so he became part of the U.S. Army **Corps** of **Engineers**. An engineer in the army was someone who would travel into the land and **survey** it. Robert helped draw the line dividing Ohio and Michigan. He also was in charge of surveying the upper Mississippi and Missouri rivers. Robert wasn't really happy as an engineer. He wanted the chance to show that he could be a great soldier, like his father.

Surveyors work on engineering projects.

17

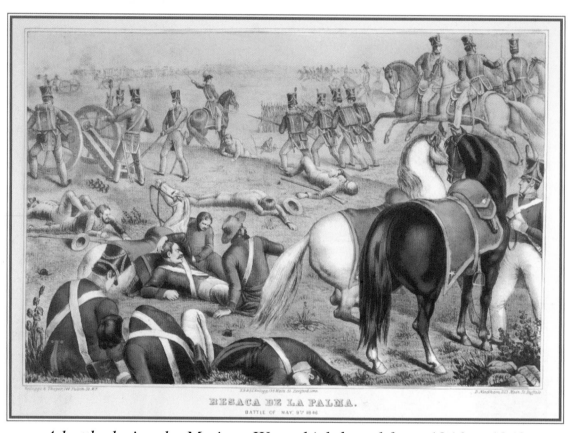

RESACA DE LA PALMA.

BATTLE OF MAY 9TH 1846

A battle during the Mexican War, which lasted from 1846 to 1848

The Mexican War

~

Robert got his chance to show what a great army officer he could be when the United States went to war with Mexico in 1846. Robert went to Texas at the start of the Mexican War.

As an engineer, Lee led scouting trips into Mexico, so soldiers would know the best way to make it through the mountains. His scouting helped the army march into Mexico City and end the war in 1847. Army reports called Robert E. Lee "the greatest military genius in America."

Texas: For almost ten years before the Mexican War, Texas was its own country. It didn't become one of the United States until 1845. Much of what is now Texas was once part of Mexico.

Back to West Point

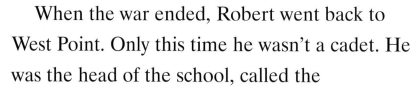

When the war ended, Robert went back to West Point. Only this time he wasn't a cadet. He was the head of the school, called the

superintendent. He spent a lot of time with the cadets. One of them, Jeb Stuart, would later be a great general with Lee in the Civil War. Beginning in 1852, Robert was superintendent of West Point for three years.

Jeb Stuart was a cadet at West Point while Lee was head of the school.

20

An engraving of Robert E. Lee, made while
he was superintendent at West Point

John Brown was against slavery.

Slaves and John Brown

During these years, there was a big disagreement in the country about **slaves**. Many people in the North felt that it should be against the law to own slaves. In the South, slaves were much more common.

One man from the North who was very much against slavery was John Brown. He went into the South, where he tried to set slaves free. In 1859, he and his men went to steal guns from the U.S. army at Harpers Ferry in what is now West Virginia. Robert E. Lee took command of the **troops** who were sent to fight John Brown. Under Lee, the troops defeated Brown and arrested him.

Harpers Ferry is a town on the Potomac River, about 50 miles (80 km) northwest of Washington, D.C.

North or South?

In 1861, the Civil War started. When the
Southern states formed the Confederate States
of America, the Northern states said they
couldn't. President Abraham Lincoln asked
Robert E. Lee to become head of the U.S. army.

Confederate and Union forces meet at the battle of Antietam.

Abraham Lincoln was president when the Civil War began.

Robert loved the United States, but he couldn't fight a war against his home state of Virginia, which had joined the Confederacy. So Robert became head of the Confederate army.

*Even though the North had more soldiers, Lee led
the South to victory at the Battle of Chancellorsville.*

A Brave Fight

~

The **Union** army of the North had more soldiers, more guns, and more money. Many times when Robert led his troops into battle, there were twice as many Union soldiers as there were Confederate soldiers. But because Robert was such a great general, his side won many of those battles. Among the biggest battles he won were the Battle of Chancellorsville and the second Battle of Bull Run.

Battle of Chancellorsville: In early May of 1863, Lee and the South won a big victory near this town in Virginia.

The South Loses

Those on both sides knew that Robert E. Lee was a great general and a fine man. But the North had the bigger and better army. Lee's troops fought bravely. When they tried to move north into Pennsylvania in 1863, they lost a big battle at Gettysburg. On April 9, 1865, the South surrendered, or gave up.

Lee surrendered to Ulysses S. Grant in 1865, and the Civil War was over.

28

The United States was one country again. The South loved Robert E. Lee, but the North also remembers him as a hero. He died on October 12, 1870.

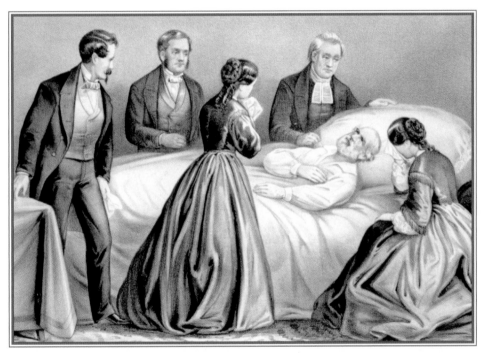

On his deathbed, Lee was surrounded by his family.

Important Dates to Remember

1807 Robert Edward Lee is born.

1818 Robert's father dies.

1825 Robert enters West Point.

1829 Robert finishes at West Point.

1846 Robert goes to Mexico to fight in the Mexican War.

1852 The U.S. Military Academy at West Point names Robert superintendent.

1859 The U.S. army sends Robert to stop John Brown at Harpers Ferry.

1861 With the start of the Civil War, Robert leaves the U.S. army and becomes head of the Confederate army.

1864 After winning many victories, the South loses the battle at Gettysburg.

1865 The North wins the Civil War.

1870 Robert E. Lee dies.

Glossary

cadets (kuh DETZ) — students at a military academy

Confederate (kon FED ur et) — a person, state or soldier on the Southern side in the Civil War

corps (KORE) — a company of people, an organized group

demerit (deh MAIR it) — a mark against someone who has broken a rule

engineers (en jin EARZ) — those who make plans and maps to measure and build

general (JEN ur ul) — the highest rank in the military

mansion (MAN shun) — a huge house

military (MILL ih TARE ee) — the armed forces

plantation (plan TAY shun) — a large farm where workers live and crops are planted and grown

slaves (SLAYVZ) — people who are owned by another person

soldiers (SOHL jerz) — those who serve in the military

superintendent (supe er in TEND ent) — the head of a system

survey (SIR vay) — explore and make a map or a plan

troops (TRUUPS) — soldiers

Union (YOON yun) — the Northern side in the Civil War

Index

Further Reading

Carter, E.J., *Robert E. Lee* (American War Biographies), Heinemann, 2004.

Grabowski, Patricia. *Robert E. Lee* (Famous Figures of the Civil War Era), Chelsea House, 2001.

King, David C. *Robert E. Lee* (Triangle Histories—the Civil War), Blackbirch Press, 2001.

Websites To Visit

http://www.americancivilwar.com/south/lee.html
http://www.robertelee.org/
http://www.nps.gov/anti/lee_bio.htm

About The Author

Don McLeese is an associate professor of journalism at the University of Iowa. He has won many awards for his journalism, and his work has appeared in numerous newspapers and magazines. He has frequently contributed to the World Book Encyclopedia and has written many books for young readers. He lives with his wife and two daughters in West Des Moines, Iowa.